PILLAR TO POST
LOOKING AT STREET FURNITURE

PILLAR TO POST

LOOKING AT STREET FURNITURE

Henry Aaron with photographs by Ian Sherren

FREDERICK WARNE · LONDON

First published by Frederick Warne (Publishers) Ltd, London, 1982
© Henry Aaron and Ian Sherren

ISBN 0 7232 2762 4

Filmset and printed in Great Britain by
BAS Printers Limited, Over Wallop, Hampshire

CONTENTS

ACKNOWLEDGEMENTS

The author wishes to thank all those who generously gave of their time and help in providing technical and other pertinent information.

Sincere thanks are also due to the staff of Frederick Warne (Publishers) Ltd, and to Ian Sherren who, with the devoted assistance of Joyce Sherren, took all the photographs. But for these, this book would never have come into existence.

JACKET ILLUSTRATIONS: (left) Village Pump, Biggar, Strathclyde (*by courtesy of the Civic Trust*); (right) Wall Letter Box, Polruan, Cornwall (*Traube Photography*)

A popular conception of a milestone is of a roughly-squared block of granite or limestone bearing in Roman numerals the mileage to some important town. In fact there is no such thing as a standardized milestone and, as the following illustrations will show, the stones and posts set up by the Romans, the turnpike trustees and by others after them exhibit an intriguing diversity of form, material, and methods of imparting information.

The milestone shown here dates from about 1751 and now stands beside the Red Rover public house in Upper Richmond Road, southwest London. That the stone bears inscriptions on all four faces indicates that it must once have stood in a more exposed position. Very considerately, a piece of glass has been let into the wall behind so that the 'back' of the stone may not be obscured. Note that a specific point (ie, the Standard in Cornhill) is mentioned, rather than just the name London and that the mileage is shown as being 'from' instead of the more usual 'to'.

So far as Britain is concerned, the practice of setting up milestones can be said to have originated with the Romans, whose skill as pioneer road builders is renowned. Though many milestones of different types must have been put up during the Roman occupation, only about a hundred have been rediscovered. Most of these are now in museums, and very few remain in situ.

The stone shown here stands near the fort of Vindolanda, Northumberland. Weathering over the centuries has reduced to a roughened state what was probably a once well-dressed cylinder and it is difficult to find any trace of the original inscription. The stone is approximately 63 in (1.6 m) high and 79 in (2 m) in girth.

After the Roman withdrawal the road system fell into decay and thus the setting up of new milestones lapsed for a considerable time. With the introduction of turnpike trusts in the eighteenth century road conditions began to improve again and the installation of milestones was made obligatory.

One of the first corporate bodies to cause the erection of a sequence of milestones was Trinity Hall, Cambridge. The series was set up between 1725 and 1735 beside the present B1368 road (Cambs/Herts) and bears the crescent emblem of the college.

The stone shown here stands by the intersection of the B1368 with the A505 and is dated 1731. There are slight variations from stone to stone in the series and this particular one is noteworthy in that it is lozenge shaped in section, and shows the directions, but not the mileages, to places other than Cambridge.

Milestones and Mileposts

Despite his notorious, and no doubt at times exaggerated, activities in the so-called Hell Fire Club and elsewhere, Sir Francis Dashwood found time to initiate a number of good works of benefit to the eighteenth-century traveller. One such act was the making of the road between High Wycombe and West Wycombe, Buckinghamshire.

At the junction of this road with that leading to Princes Risborough stands this unique columnar milestone dated MDCCLII (1752). In a clockwise direction the inscriptions below the ball read:

From the city miles XXX
From the county town miles XV
From the university miles XXII

This milestone is one of a series standing beside the A30 road between Salisbury and Shaftesbury. The principal point of interest is that these stones bear the somewhat enigmatic words Sarum and Shaston, the contractions of the two towns' respective medieval Latin names.

Even more enigmatic than the A30 milestones between Salisbury and Shaftesbury are the wordless mileposts standing beside the A22 road in East Sussex. These iron posts, supported in their old age by wooden posts, depict four bells and a bow (ie, Bow bells) signifying London, the mileage thereto (or from), and a buckle, the badge of the Pelham family, who held considerable estates in the district.

The hollow iron milepost shown here is one of a series standing beside the A427 road in Leicestershire. Made at Joseph Illston's Victory Foundry in Leicester, and dating probably from the early nineteenth century, the posts are not over attractive, but are nevertheless distinctly unusual insofar as they bear a royal coat of arms now rather blurred by clumsy painting.

Not all mileage markers were of stone. Cast iron was also used in the past to make posts of many different shapes and sizes. Particularly distinctive in style are the posts standing beside roads in the Bakewell and Buxton areas of Derbyshire. These posts made by at least two foundries in Derby date from about 1880 and are noteworthy in that the placename London is cast, whereas the names of other places were painted on as local requirements dictated. This brilliant idea could have led to the posts being used virtually anywhere in Britain but because publicity and marketing were not then highly organized, the design did not achieve the success it deserved.

But for one outstanding feature the meeting place of the A44 and B4081 roads in Gloucestershire would have the appearance of many an ordinary country crossroads. Its claim to fame is that it is the site of what may well be the oldest finger signs still in situ in Britain. They are dated 1669 and no earlier signs have yet been found.

The narrow iron fingers (rather out of proportion to the tall, white-painted wooden post on which they are now mounted) are inscribed on both sides. The directions, reading clockwise, are:

XXIIII MILES 1669
THE WAY TO OXFORD
XVIII MILES N I (Nicholas Izold)
THE WAY TOG LOSTER (sic)

XVI MILES N I
THE WAY TO WOSTER (sic)
XV MILES 1669
THE WAY TO WARWICK

Not so very far from Izold's signpost is the sign known as Teddington Hands, near Teddington, Gloucestershire. This six-fingered, octagonal pillar of local stone bears a duplicated inscription in poor verse describing its erection by 'Edmund Attwood of the Vine Tree.' No date is shown, but the pillar is reputedly seventeenth-century.

To meet the demands of modern traffic the roads hereabouts have been realigned to converge on the roundabout in the background of this picture. As a result Attwood's pillar, which once stood at a crossroads, has now lost much of its former significance.

The reinforced concrete signpost standing at Bassett's Pole, Staffordshire, is certainly not so old as Izold's sign, but it does stand on an historic site. As recorded on a tablet at the base of the post, Lord Bassett of Drayton set up a boundary pole here 'in the reign of King John and the year of Our Lord 1201.'

It is sad to relate that with the realignment of routes in the vicinity the signpost has become more or less discarded amongst disjointed bits of road now used as an illicit dumping ground for rubbish.

Dorset possesses an odd sign beside the A31 road near Bere Regis. Although of a once fairly commonplace type, the sign is remarkable in that both post and boards are painted red. The placenames are made up of white-painted screw-on letters and the 'W's on the lower boards signify Winterborne in the names of the three places so prefixed.

The sign has been augmented by a more modern one on the other side of the road, but the distances shown do not agree in every case. The spot, known as Red Post, may once have been the site of a gibbet, but the derivation of the name is obscure.

The counties of Cumbria, Dorset and Yorkshire have in common the use of signposts bearing the grid references for their individual positions; a generous if but little-used gesture towards the traveller.

The signpost shown here displays not only its grid reference, but also the name of the place. Bedlam as a placename is not altogether unusual and may sometimes indicate the past existence of an asylum or hospital in the neighbourhood. The legend 'Yorks. W.R.' signifies the former West Riding of Yorkshire, since 1974 called West Yorkshire.

The granite guidestone here shown stands beside an unclassified road near Stoke Climsland, Cornwall. It dates from about 1762 and its portrayal of the four pointing hands is a particularly fascinating feature.

Because of their relative permanence many milestones have in the past been incised with the Ordnance Survey bench mark. This guidestone too has been so marked, on its north side, below the pointer to Bray Shop.

On the opposite side of the road from the granite guidestone illustrated on page 14 is this more recent aid for the unsure traveller. The individual boards are excellent examples of their kind but the proximity of the two signs invites unfavourable comparison of the agglomeration of finger signs with the simplicity of the older guidestone.

Certain counties have in the past adopted their own distinctive styles of signpost. Such individuality is pleasing, but is unfortunately becoming rarer as old signs are displaced by new display-type boards.

One example of a local style is Hampshire's use of signs having a row of pointed studs along the top edge. It has been stated that the purpose of the studs is, or was, to discourage swinging from the signposts' arms, though why the natives of Hampshire in particular should be disposed to this frivolity remains a mystery.

In the early days of motoring the erection of roadside signs was to some extent brought about by both local and national organizations formed to help the amateur driver. These signs could be of an informatory or a warning nature and one such is shown here. It gives not only the placename but also a mild warning to take care.

Investigations have failed to reveal conclusively what the initials H.A.C. stand for. However it is highly probable that they are those of the Herefordshire Automobile Club, which was founded in 1903 and certainly undertook as one of its functions the erection of roadside warning signs.

Placename Signs

Characteristic of Lancashire before the redrawing of county boundaries in 1974 were the roadside signs that proclaimed the name of a town or village and the number of the road on which it stood. Such a sign is that shown here, which in announcing the name Hoole does duty for Little Hoole and Much Hoole (both of which remain in the reshaped county).

There are numerous ways in which placenames may be exhibited. These range from the prosaic and unadorned nameboard to the truly decorative, often found in places which take a pride in their appearance or history.

Many Yorkshire villages display their names in attractive fashion by using a stone-built trough of flowers or a redundant millstone as a support for the nameboard. An example of the latter practice is the millstone at Rievaulx, North Yorkshire, shown here; glass reflectors are used to pick out each letter.

Placename Signs

If well designed, a sign in silhouette or outline made from sheet or wrought metal can be very attractive. A particularly good one is that standing beside the A30 road on the outskirts of Milborne Port, Somerset. The sign was erected in 1970 and depicts the parish church of St John the Evangelist, and a waterwheel representative of past industry in the area.

Bedfordshire possesses some beautiful villages whose attractiveness is matched by the local style of nameboard. Painted in black and cream, these boards bear decorative roundels showing the county coat of arms and the emblem of the 1951 Festival of Britain, a Britannia and pennants motif.

Placename Signs

Some towns erect near their boundaries nameboards which proudly portray a famous building or event associated with the locality. Typical of this type of board are those standing on the outskirts of Ledbury in the county of Hereford and Worcester. The painting shows the town's notable seventeenth-century market hall.

East Anglia, an area of many charming villages and few large towns, is also remarkable for its high incidence of village signs which are probably thicker on the ground here than anywhere else in Britain. Many of these signs are of the post and picture type, but one of the more unusual is that standing on the green in Earl Soham, Suffolk.

The village was once the residence of falconers to the Dukes of Norfolk and the figure depicted is that of an anonymous falconer. The sign was carved by students of Ipswich Art School and erected by the local Women's Institute in 1953 to commemorate the coronation of Elizabeth II.

In certain parts of Britain a number of towns and villages have adopted a style of nameboard that is peculiar to the locality. A particularly distinctive type of board is that used by the member towns of the Cinque Ports in East Sussex and Kent. Shown here is a sign standing on the outskirts of Lydd, Kent, whose name, as a matter of incidental interest, gave rise to that of the explosive Lyddite.

Although once fairly commonplace, little use has been made within the last 50 years of blue and white enamelled plates to display road and street names. So long as it remains in situ, this example is to be seen in Southport, Merseyside.

Birmingham has much to show the street furniture enthusiast. Particularly distinctive are the old cast-iron road name signs reminiscent in form of chemists' scales. The sign shown here is of a type having a finial at the top; but another, almost identical, design has above the nameplate a scroll motif instead of the spike.

The post is semicircular in section, a feature that allows it to be positioned close to a wall or other vertical surface. There are, however, in the city a number of similar semicircular posts standing free of walls and other encumbrances.

This cast-iron sign in Finchley, north London, is interesting because of the addition of the postal district number on a separate plate. However, it should not be assumed that the road sign predates the introduction of postal district numbers, for on the opposite side of the road both street name and postal district appear together on a sign of similar construction and therefore probably of similar date.

Road Name Signs

Peculiar to parts of Nottingham is the use of circular signs to exhibit street names. Rather oddly, some of these, on posts taller than that shown here, stand in residents' gardens.

A T-shaped precast concrete support forms the very practical setting for this road name in Hatfield, Hertfordshire. The concrete itself requires virtually no maintenance and is resistant to all but the more severe of blows.

Road Name Signs

One of the more unusual forms of road sign is that peculiar to the St Budeaux district of Plymouth. Somewhat after the fashion of swinging inn signs, those of St Budeaux each comprise a cast-iron plate suspended from a frame at the top of a concrete or timber post.

Whereas the majority of these signs exhibit merely the road name, this one, at the top of Normandy Hill, gives a scrap of significant history by recording that it was US army route number 23 for the allied D-day invasion of France in June 1944.

Ceramic tiles bearing individual letters have been used in the past to display road names in a way that seems to add a note of distinction to the neighbourhood concerned. Favoured colours include black, blue, brown, and red, either as a background colour with the letters white, or for the letters themselves upon a white background. For some reason such tiles appear to be less subject to vandalism than are other types of sign and they deserve to be used more extensively. The fine example shown here was photographed in Torquay, Devon.

The classification and numbering of roads on a national basis was begun in 1922. On a smaller scale roads within the new town of Milton Keynes, Buckinghamshire, which in their early days tended to be rather featureless and similar in appearance, have been given numbers as an added means of identification.

Although extremely neat in design, low-standing signs such as this one may easily be temporarily obscured by passing vehicles.

Up to the nineteenth century street furniture was by no means so abundant as it is today. For the long-distance traveller in those far-off times one of the more gruesome sights would have been the gibbet or gallows. Gibbets were often set up at crossroads, at parish boundaries, or on prominent hills, and in the days when hanging was an all too frequent penalty the victims might be left dangling for a week or more.

A few gibbets survive, notably on Inkpen Beacon, Berkshire, and at Steng Cross, Northumberland, but it is questionable how much of the original fabrics remain. This one stands beside the A14 road in Cambridgeshire, and is known as Caxton Gibbet.

Because of its insulation by heavy traffic the majority of passers-by are probably oblivious of the existence of this commemorative stone. Set in an island at the frenetic Marble Arch end of London's Edgware Road, the limestone plaque marks the alleged site of the onetime dreaded Tyburn gallows. The precise spot is in fact uncertain.

Pillories are these days sufficiently rare to merit more than a passing glance. This particularly fine specimen used to stand in the market place in Coleshill, Warwickshire, and was moved to its present position in Church Hill in 1865. It is also of more than usual interest (and may well be unique) in that it combines in one structure a double pillory, whipping post, and stocks.

The former county of Rutland, now absorbed into Leicestershire, possessed some delightful towns and villages, not least among which is Market Overton. Attractive old buildings cluster around a tidy little green on which stand the combined stocks and whipping post. Both green and stocks are well kept and their good condition is an example of what can be achieved.

A case for care. Although the wheeled stocks in Bilton, Warwickshire, are not unique (another example exists in Colne, Lancashire), they are nevertheless rare enough to deserve better maintenance.

The village of Duddingston in Lothian possesses a number of interesting features including a venerable kirk, a mounting block and, attached to the churchyard wall, this old iron neckband known locally as the jougs. The band was used to hold captive those found guilty of minor offences and its short chain that enforced a standing position can have allowed the culprit little comfort or movement.

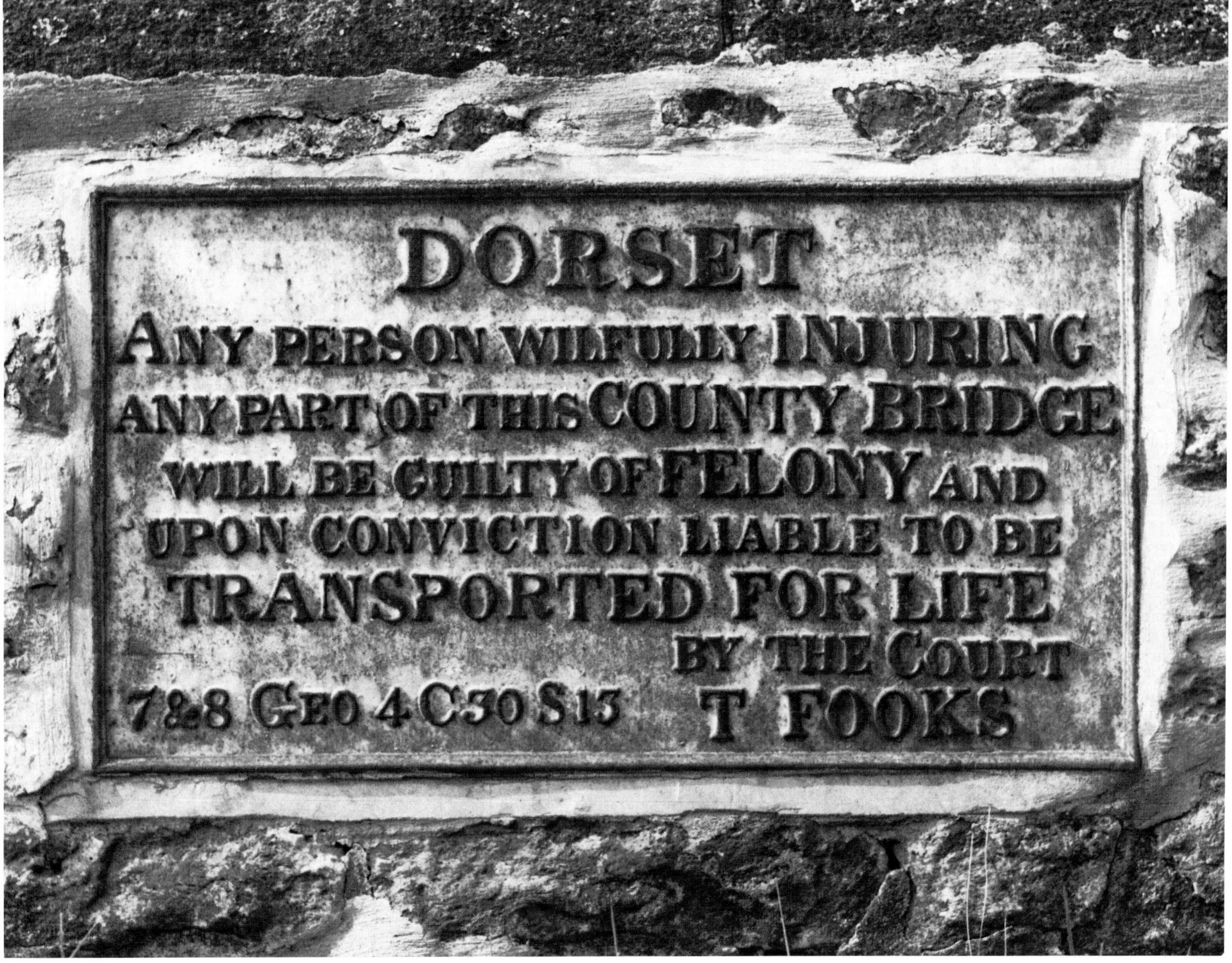

Up to the third and fourth decades of the nineteenth century severe penalties were imposed for what would nowadays be regarded as minor offences; until the 1830s many crimes were punishable by hanging or transportation.

As this cast-iron plate on a bridge over the River Lydden near Kingstag, Dorset, still testifies, in the reign of George IV transportation for life could have been imposed for wilfully damaging a county bridge.

The ornate but now slightly dilapidated drinking fountain shown here is attached to a wall on the Castle Esplanade, Edinburgh. Designed by John Duncan and dated 1894, it serves as a memorial to the many alleged witches who, whether or not guilty of any misdemeanour, were burned to death nearby.

Up to the end of the nineteenth century the horse served as the principal form of motive power. With the coming of the internal combustion engine the horse's role began to decline until today it is rare to see a horse on the road used for other than police or recreational purposes.

The extensive employment of horses in the past brought about related items of street furniture which are now outmoded or very little used. One such piece of furniture is the mounting block, remaining examples of which are best sought outside churches and old inns. The aged example shown here, apparently incorporating the living rock, stands outside the churchyard in Duddingston, Lothian.

This fine stone-built block, standing beside the churchyard wall in Bradwell-on-Sea, Essex, is noteworthy for the unusual iron post on its top step.

A close-up of the beautifully shaped iron post on the top step of the Bradwell-on-Sea mounting block.

This awesome drinking trough stands beside the High Street in the centre of Chipping Sodbury, Avon. As may be seen, the side facing the pavement bears an incisive portrayal of Queen Victoria. That facing the road bears details of the trough's presentation to the town as a memorial of the Queen's diamond jubilee in 1897. It is interesting to speculate on the considerations that may have governed the decision as to which way round these adornments should be placed.

Though many drinking troughs still remain in situ the majority no longer contain water and, if not filled in, have tended to degenerate into receptacles for litter. In some cases, as at Chipping Sodbury, they have been made into attractive flower beds.

The Metropolitan Drinking Fountain and Cattle Trough Association was founded, as the Metropolitan Free Drinking Fountain Association, in 1859. The Association's original aim was to set up drinking fountains for public use but within a few years it was also encouraging the provision of roadside drinking troughs for cattle and horses which at times were hard pressed by their owners and drivers.

Nearly a thousand M.D.F & C.T.A. troughs have been set up in Britain and overseas and of these about half were in the London area. The heavy granite troughs may still be seen in some numbers although more often than not they no longer hold water. An exception is this trough in Hyde Park, London, which, if no longer used by draught horses, is at least used occasionally by those being ridden in the park.

Like many other old market towns, Market Harborough in Leicestershire has a wide street in which animals and produce were formerly sold and bought. Unique to Market Harborough, however, are the three ranges of kerbside posts to which animals, or at least horses, used to be tethered. Now they are occasionally used for tying up the shopper's dog. The three ranges differ in style; the post shown here belongs to a group of four, and bears the ascription 'John Law Leicester'.

If a road traverses an area where cattle or sheep are left to graze, gates or grids may be placed across the road to prevent the animals from wandering too far. Road gates may be troublesome and expensive to keep in good condition, and impatient drivers may be tempted to leave them open. By comparison cattle grids are relatively maintenance-free and, whilst deterring stock from straying, allow the motorist to go on his way unhindered.

Typical of the grids to be encountered in the more remote parts of Britain is this one on the B4355 Welsh mountain road between Dolfor and Felindre in Powys.

In an attempt to deter deer from running into the road in the path of oncoming traffic the Forestry Commission has experimented with the use of red reflectors to catch the headlights of passing vehicles.

The example shown here is one of a series standing beside the A337 road between Brockenhurst and Lyndhurst in the New Forest, a particularly busy and straight stretch where drivers are tempted to speed. The plastic reflectors are produced in Austria and are attached to timber posts at intervals of approximately 50 ft (15 m) along each side of the road. Similar methods have been tried on Great Haldon, Devon, and in Richmond Park, southwest London.

In the early eighteenth century the spa of Bath was growing in popularity and elegance. Beau Nash the gambler and self-made ruler of Bath did much to improve social behaviour and encourage building in the town.

Nash is also credited with having caused the erection of pumps alongside the road between London and Bath. In those days the road was but a glorified track and men were employed to lay the dust by sprinkling it with water obtained from the pumps. A number of pumps may still be seen beside the A4 road between Theale, Berkshire, and Marlborough, Wiltshire. Not unnaturally, they are now in rather a decayed condition; one of the better examples is this one near Thatcham, Berkshire.

It is easy to lose sight of the fact that the vast conurbation that is London has grown from an amalgam of old towns and villages. Many of these no doubt once had communal conduits, pumps, or wells, to provide a supply of water to the populace. Few such facilities now remain.

Aldgate pump at the junction of Fenchurch Street and Leadenhall Street in the City of London is a late nineteenth-century structure of stone standing on or near the site of an ancient well. Though no longer operative, the pump retains a beautiful brass spout variously described as being the head of a dog, fox, or wolf.

It may also be of interest to mention that the saying 'A draught' (draft) 'on Aldgate pump' was formerly used to signify something worthless.

In addition to its two Victorian letter boxes (see page 106), Framlingham in Suffolk has an aged water pump of interest to the connoisseur. As pumps go it is a rather massive thing with two spouts and a height of 8 ft (2.4 m). The lower spout was for domestic use whilst the larger was intended for such purposes as filling the thirsty tanks of traction engines, water carts, and the like. The pump shown here apparently bears no indication as to its makers and little is known about its age except that it is at least one hundred years old.

Water Supply

A plaque on the side of this green-painted pump in the village of Stanton by Dale, Derbyshire, proclaims that it was 'Erected in loyal commemoration of the beneficent reign of Queen Victoria June 22nd. 1897. The gift of the women of Stanton'.

Although Derbyshire has no mean reputation in the field of iron work, on this occasion the ladies of Stanton did not support local industry for the pump clearly bears the name 'Coalbrookdale'.

It will be noticed that at some time since 1897 the trough, bowls and overflow gully have all been filled in.

This attractive cast-iron standpipe stands beside the main road that passes through the village of Maxton, Borders. It was made by the well-known producers of such equipment, Glenfield & Kennedy Ltd of Kilmarnock, Strathclyde, but the domestic-style tap is of course a more recent addition.

An extremely simple, practical, and rare style of standpipe in the Devonshire village of Aveton Gifford, which possesses two, and possibly the only two, examples of the kind.

Standpipes made by Glenfield & Kennedy Ltd of Kilmarnock are not uncommon; but not all are now in so good a state of preservation as this one in Ditherington, Shropshire. Painted a light blue, the standpipe is unusual in bearing the legend 'Waste not want not'.

Contrary to American practice, relatively few fire hydrants have been erected in the streets of British cities and towns. One notable exception was in Nottingham, although the hydrants there have now been disconnected and can in consequence no longer be used. Prior to their disconnection use was made of the pillars for filling water carts as well as for fire-fighting purposes. About 50 such hydrants of slightly varying patterns and all painted red remain standing about the city. The example shown here is approximately 67 in (170 cm) tall and stands in Queens Road, NG2.

Early pavement posts were often fashioned from old cannon adapted for the purpose, or were specially made in their likeness complete with ball protruding from the muzzle.

As befits an important naval town, Portsmouth possesses cannon dating from the eighteenth century in some of the older streets. In their rusting old age it is frequently difficult to date cannon with accuracy, but the twelve-pounder shown here, which stands in Tower Street, has, rightly or wrongly, had the year 1708 added to a trunnion.

This octagonal iron bollard stands just off Lower Thames Street in the City of London. It dates from the reign of George IV (1820–30) and a crown and the monogram IIII GR are discernible on its south side.

Southwark in south London was in the past notorious for its inns, prisons, prostitutes and theatres. The encouragement of at least some of these has been attributed to the presence of the London palace of the bishops of Winchester and its liberty called the Clink. As is well known, the slang word clink is synonymous with prison. Today the name is perpetuated by Clink Street, and by a quantity of bollards in the area which bear the date 1821 or 1826.

This cube-headed bollard stands on the perimeter of the station yard in Buxton, Derbyshire, and is dated 1864.

A visit to Ironbridge in Shropshire is a must for tourists and those interested in industrial archaeology. The Iron Bridge itself, the World's first, and the nearby Coalbrookdale ironworks are, of course, the principal attractions, but the town has many other intriguing features. Not unnaturally, the place also possesses an assortment of iron furniture not all of which is of local manufacture. The cast-iron bollard shown here stands near the Tontine Hotel and is one of a number of mixed vintage that stud the pavements in the area.

An interesting pair of dissimilar iron pavement posts in Carpenters Arms Lane, Newport, Gwent.

One of a rank of five similar posts standing in the market place in Cambridge. Slightly smaller than the average bollard, this cream-painted post is exquisitely proportioned and bears the inscription 'Headly & Edwards Ltd Cambridge'.

The hollow iron bollard standing on a traffic island beside the A43 road shown here is one of a type that may easily disappear altogether from the roads in Northampton. Unfortunately little is known regarding the make and precise age of these posts (painted either black-and-white or green-and-white), but they may date from around the very end of the nineteenth century.

It will be noted that the design follows less closely that of old cannon, but the semblance of a cannon ball at the top has been retained.

What is it?

Probably the passage of innumerable boots and shoes has, over the years, worn smooth this semicircular plate measuring approximately 14 in (35 cm) across and set in the pavement in Smithdown Road, Liverpool. The chances are that it once bore the inscription 'Boundary post L. & N. W. Ry. Co.'. If so, it must date from sometime between the company's formation in 1846 and its absorption in 1923 when Britain's railways were amalgamated into four main groups. More precisely it may date from about 1888 when the nearby railway line was widened.

An extremely interesting and rare example of a pavior's advertisement set in a pavement in the Scots town of Haddington, Lothian. Stuarts Granolithic was founded in 1840; the company still flourishes but no longer uses this pavement sign.

The Cambridge enigma. There is a slight chance that these brass letters could be all that remain of a paving maker's advertisement. Set in the pavement at the junction of Green Street and Sidney Street, Cambridge, and $2\frac{1}{2}$ in (6.5 cm) high, it is perhaps more likely that they once formed part of the street name. If so it is indeed a rare, if not unique, way of displaying a street name.

One of several finely formed brass numbers screwed to the kerbing in various parts of Wimbledon, southwest London. Their actual age is uncertain, and their use must have mystified many.

The number 'twenty-one' shown here is in St Mark's Place and the purpose of this and of others elsewhere is to act as reference numbers for licensed street traders.

Discovery of the unexpected contributes much to the pleasures of the seeker after street furniture. An iron railing in Trendle Street, Sherborne, Dorset, provides some protection for pedestrians on the narrow pavement. Each of its supporting posts is capped with a simulated bishop's mitre, and the railing might therefore be thought to date from the appointment in 1925 of the first suffragan bishop of Sherborne. In fact it is more likely to date from about 1866, the mitre being the badge of the nearby almshouse, which was extended at that time.

The days are gone when it was not unusual to see men and boys carrying heavy loads along the street. Out of compassion for the porter's lot, R. A. Slaney, MP for Shrewsbury, had this rest erected in Piccadilly, Westminster, in 1861. As the plate explains, it is 'for the benefit of porters and others carrying burdens'. It is also unique.

Many towns and cities now have guided walks marked in various ways. An example is shown here of the unobtrusive guided walkway markers fixed in some quantity to the pavements of the City of London.

Pavements

Perhaps not the most beautiful item of street furniture to be seen in Britain. This silver-coloured and very conspicuous device was erected in 1977 in Great George Street, Westminster, and serves as an assembly point marker for the Silver Jubilee Walkway.

Of all the different types of hole cover that abound in the streets of Britain coal plates are probably the most fascinating. They are of many patterns, and, unlike much street furniture, frequently bear the name and address of their makers. Among the more prolific of these were the Haywards of Borough, in southeast London.

At a hasty glance the trademark on this worn coal plate looks like an old-fashioned coal scuttle which would be particularly apt. However, on more careful examination it will be seen that it is actually the representation of a padlock. The plate itself is comparatively ancient and may well date from the 1850s or 1860s.

One of the more prolific producers of coal plates was T. Sampson of Euston Road, northwest London. Sampson made both solid and attractively perforated plates such as that shown here, which is approximately 12 in (30 cm) in diameter.

The holes admit a modicum of light into the cellar but also encourage the entry of dirt and rain. As a counter measure the householder could perhaps have hung up an enamelled bowl on chains as has been done en masse in at least one underground lavatory that has a perforated skylight in the pavement.

Coal plates in an assortment of designs and sizes were also made by Hayward's of Borough in southeast London. In this example of their work the design is approximately 14 in (35.5 cm) in diameter, is self-locking, and has four, now much abraded, glass lights. The ring holding the plate bears the inscription 'This ring to be fixed with Portland cement for Haywards patent plate 14 in.' The instruction does not appear to have been strictly adhered to, for some of these rings can be seen holding plates of other makes.

On the north side of Charlotte Square, Edinburgh, which is still largely Georgian in character, a slightly elevated pavement is separated from the road by a bank of sloping flagstones. Set rather unusually on the tilt are a number of covers giving access to the cellars of the adjacent houses. The cover shown here was made by Mackenzie & Moncur Ltd of Edinburgh, who have been responsible for a great deal of the city's street furniture.

The history of London's gas supply industry may be partially traced by the different initials to be seen on valve covers set in its pavements. The World's first gas supply company, the Chartered Gas Light and Coke Company, came into being in 1812, and the well-worn cover shown here bears the initials 'GLCC'. With the advent of nationalization in 1949, the GLCC was absorbed into the North Thames Gas Board whose initials 'NTGB' now appear on many covers.

The iron cover shown above was discovered set in the pavement bordering the boat pool in Dartmouth, Devon. Dartmouth has never had a railway station of its own and has had to rely on a ferry service connecting with the one-time GWR (now Dart Valley Light Railway Company) Kingswear station on the opposite bank of the river. The Great Western Railway penetrated into south Devon in the latter part of the nineteenth century and it would not be unreasonable to suppose that this rare cover dates from about that time.

The most frequently encountered types of hole cover include the coal plate, Post Office jointing pit cover, and hydrant cover. Examples of the last are best seen in built-up areas where they are usually set in the pavement at more or less regular intervals, and frequently at street corners. Among suppliers of such covers whose products have been extensively used are: J. Blakeborough & Son of Brighouse, West Yorkshire; Guest & Chrimes of Rotherham, South Yorkshire; and Ham Baker & Co Ltd of Westminster.

The telephone system in Britain was initially built up by the Post Office and a number of private companies working under licence. One such leading company was the National Telephone Company from which the Post Office took over in 1912.

Few readily-identifiable relics of the NTC remain. It was therefore a pleasant surprise to find the pit cover shown here on The Mound, Edinburgh. Bearing the legend 'National Telephone Co Ltd', it resides unobtrusively in a sequence of more common Post Office covers and probably goes unnoticed by the many thousands of pedestrians who trudge up and down the hill.

A field of study that has not yet received the attention it deserves is that of service indicator plates and posts. Their age and make can all too often be only guessed at but the very many different patterns used throughout Britain are worthy of examination, not least for the different ways in which they impart their information. From the enthusiast's point of view it is a pity that this variety is being lost; metrication has led to the replacement of many signs, the new ones being nearly always metal plates on concrete posts.

Unfortunately little is known about the make and age of the indicator plate in Buxton, Derbyshire, shown here. Even so, its intriguing shield-like shape and the use of dots to differentiate between feet and inches make it of more than average interest.

The use of signs to indicate the presence of stopcocks for fire-fighting purposes dates back to the year 1707 when an Act of Parliament made them obligatory. Since then many varieties of painted, enamelled, and cast signs have been used. Often they bear the words 'Fire plug', 'Fire hydrant', or 'Hydrant', or for short the initials 'FP', 'FH', or 'H'. Coloration is usually black and yellow or, in older types, blue and white or red and white.

The enamelled plate shown here is one of a type once common in the cities of London and Westminster. In white on a red background, the combined letters H and D signify a double hydrant. Note that no indication whatsoever is given as to the vital distance of the hydrant from the plate!

The wall plate shown here is one of several in and around Sherborne, Dorset. This type of plate is unusual in having a disc of glass reflectors to help emphasize its presence after dark. Many of the reflectors have become broken and one had been painted over in conventional fire hydrant yellow. The figures denoting the distance in feet and inches of the hydrant from the plate were made separately or painted on, and varied on different plates according to the location.

In affectionate memory of the late Burton Latimer Water Works.

This very explicit and possibly unique indicator post stands on the outskirts of Burton Latimer, Northamptonshire, and shows the distances to an assortment of valves.

With the sporadic advance of metrication, old indicator plates bearing measurements in feet and inches are now gradually being replaced by new signs giving metric measurements. The concrete post shown here, one of many in the Mill Hill area of north London, carries a plate with a black letter H on a reflective yellow background, and is a good example of the new type.

Plates marking the proximity of a valve in an underground gas pipe are considerably rarer than those indicating a valve in a water pipe. The enamelled plate shown here is attached to railings in Charlotte Square, Edinburgh. The coloration is red on a white background, and the figure 18 betokens a lateral distance of 18 ft (5 m) to a valve in the road.

The laying down of trunk gas pipelines throughout the country has led to the widespread use of markers to indicate the presence of a buried pipe. The markers normally take the form of a white painted post with a bright red cap that sometimes bears a reference number in black. Many but not all such posts occur at the roadside where they may serve to mark where a road crosses a pipe.

From an enviromental point of view the buried pipe, the pipeline indicator, and the occasional gas sub-station, compare favourably with electricity pylons that stride conspicuously across town and country.

Before concrete posts came into general use the Post Office employed hollow iron posts to indicate the presence of jointing points in its underground cables. The standard length between points was 176 yd (160 m) and posts normally occurred at about that frequency.

The post shown here stood beside the A390 road in Tywardreath Highway, Cornwall, and marked a joint in the telegraph cable between London and the Porthcurno radio station, this section of which was laid down in 1908–09.

Although this type of post may yet be seen fairly often standing beside some of our older main roads it would be exceptional to find one on which the numbers of feet and inches were still marked.

Street lighting cannot be regarded as having been very effective before gas lamps on free-standing posts were first brought into use in 1807. Before that time those who chose or were obliged to move about after dark might have carried a lantern or had to rely on the light emanating from windows or an occasional lamp attached to a building. In the eighteenth century the well-to-do town dweller might hire a linkman or boy to carry a flaming torch ahead of him in the none-too-safe streets. Evidence of this practice survives in some of the more refined parts of Bath, Edinburgh and London, where many an elegant town house is still graced by the extinguisher (sometimes erroneously referred to as a snuff) used by the linkman to put out his torch.

Shown here and overleaf are representatives of two types of extinguisher to be seen in Edinburgh: the more usual cone-shaped variety in Charlotte Square . . .

. . . and the defiant-looking snake in Melville Street. It is interesting to note that these extinguishers are positioned at heights of about 60 and 42 in (1.5 m and 1 m) respectively, whereas those in London tend to be placed higher.

It is a noticeable fact that houses in the older and more select streets of many towns and cities are often used as places of practice by professional people such as accountants, doctors, and solicitors. It is also noticeable that these streets are inclined to retain at least some of the trappings associated with an earlier age.

Rodney Street in Liverpool is a typical example. The first house there was put up in about 1783 and much remains from the ensuing years including the now derelict church and nineteenth-century gas lamps with their distinctive ventilators. The lamps, one of which is shown here, have since been converted to electricity, but even so the use of semi-opaque glass for the lanterns seems out of keeping.

The Webb Patent Sewer Gas Destructor was an ingenious type of street lamp that burnt off gas conducted by a pipe within the post itself from an obliging sewer below pavement level. Although once fairly numerous, few examples now remain. This fine specimen stands at the junction of Lord Street and Portland Street in Southport, Merseyside. Note the particularly long ladder rests and also the local style of oval service indicator plates attached to the low wall behind the lamp post.

Gas-burning street lamps that still operate are now sadly rare. Outside London one of the best places to see working gas lamps is the Park Estate in Nottingham. The majority of lamps here are of one style with three mantles and slight tulip-like decoration on the posts themselves. The diminutive ladder rests should be compared with those of the sewer lamp on page 92. Although these Nottingham posts look similar, they were made by a variety of companies, including Humphreys & Eyer Ltd and W. White & Son (both of Nottingham) and Meadow Foundry Co Ltd of Mansfield.

In these days of mass-produced lighting standards it is refreshing to encounter older posts showing a marked degree of individuality. It is even more gratifying to discover a lamp that is unique. One such stands near the junction of Slough Road and Common Lane in Eton, Berkshire. The lantern is supported by a delicately wrought outburst of floral decoration standing on a stepped stone base. Known locally as the Burning Bush, the lamp, shown here, dates from 1864.

Probably more statues and memorials have been erected in honour of Queen Victoria than of any other person living or dead. Her diamond jubilee in 1897 gave rise to a spate of commemoration and one of the more agreeable products to survive is this street lamp in Probus, Cornwall. Not only is it a useful adjunct but it is also a pleasant thing to behold.

In Scotland and, to a lesser extent, in the north of England lamps were sometimes set up outside buildings of local importance and the homes of some civic dignitaries. Often these lamps are surmounted with crowns, executed in varying degrees of thoroughness and detail.

The pair of lamps shown here stand outside the Chambers Institution in the High Street of Peebles in Scotland. Their points of interest include the rudimentary crowns, the exceptional shape of the lantern, with its glass bearing the town arms, and the posts painted in dark red and silver.

A little neglected, and largely ignored by passers-by, the blue-painted street orderly bin shown here stood beside the southern approach to Tower Bridge in London. It deserved more than a passing glance.

The bin was undated but may reasonably be assumed to date from about the time of the bridge's opening in 1894. In those days, before mechanical sweeping became the norm, an army of street sweepers was employed to clean the streets of rubbish, remove prodigious amounts of horse droppings, and grit or sand the roads when slippery. The bin bore the name of John Knox & Co London Ltd.

Characteristic of Birmingham are the roadside litter bins, one of which is shown here. The bins (removable, either officially or otherwise!) are made of plastic and the stands of metal. Regrettably many of the bins are now missing.

In their denuded state the stands are very reminiscent of the porters' rest in Piccadilly, Westminster (see page 70), and in fact the platform-like top does offer a convenient resting place for shopping or shopper.

This fine cast-iron box in Friar Gate, Derby, formerly served as housing for an electrical transformer. Carefully painted in blue and red, it was made by W. Macfarlane & Co Ltd of Glasgow, and bears entwined figures which appear to form the year 1893. The box stands not far from the magnificent old railway bridge, spanning Friar Gate, made by Andrew Handyside & Co of Derby.

Not every item of street furniture receives floral tribute such as does this electricity supply box located on a roundabout in Southport, Merseyside. The makers were A. Handyside & Co Ltd of Derby, probably better known to street furniture enthusiasts as producers of letter boxes.

For the street furniture enthusiast any object that bears a date is especially valuable, since it can thus be put into correct historical perspective. Unfortunately few roadside objects bear any positive indication of their age, which can only sometimes be established by exhaustive search into old records.

This street lighting box in Ealing, west London, however, very clearly bears the date 1911, just 30 years after the first multiple use of incandescent street lamps. Painted dark green and tending to rust, this particular box (which would contain a time switch and cables) now has its door kept more or less shut by a piece of encircling wire.

The first half of this century was the heyday of the electric tram, when many towns and cities throughout Britain operated extensive and sometimes efficient services.

Among these was Portsmouth, blessed with an almost level system using overhead transmission. A few relics from this system survive, notably in the Cosham and Fratton areas, but their future is uncertain. These remains include old passenger shelters (one of which is illustrated on page 140), a quantity of poles that once supported the overhead wires, and the silver-painted and now derelict junction box in Cosham shown here. It bears the legend Corporation Tramways 1901 and stands next to one of several redundant traction poles.

One of a pair of heavy iron hoods covering fire hydrants in the legal enclave of the Middle Temple, City of London. The hoods appear to bear no trace of their maker's name and their age is uncertain; but they are probably contemporary with the adjacent buildings which date from the early 1880s.

The vase-like handle on the top is of a style to be found echoed on iron railings elsewhere. For many years the hoods were green in colour but shortly after this photograph was taken they were repainted in black.

(Photograph reproduced by the permission of the Honourable Society of the Middle Temple.)

This unique and mystifying dark green structure in Rupert Street, Bristol, provides access to the River Frome which passes underground hereabouts. The top of the column is open to the sky, thereby providing some light down below.

Most kerbside furniture is liable to be damaged by traffic and passers-by. The Bristol box is no exception in this respect. On at least one occasion it had to be removed, but was repaired and reinstated.

Despite its size and colour, the box has apparently been mistaken for a letter box; someone was once seen trying to post a letter in it.

Roadside pillar boxes were first introduced in Jersey in 1852 and to England in 1853. Since that date letter boxes in many different styles have become a very familiar sight in the streets of Britain and their numbers now total about 100,000.

The oldest pillar box still in use in Britain stands near Barnes Cross, Dorset, and, as befits so historic an artefact, it is maintained in fine condition. The makers of the octagonal box were John M. Butt & Co. of Gloucester, and it dates from about 1853.

Framlingham in Suffolk has two octagonal letter boxes dating from about 1856. They are of the same type but possess minor individual differences. As in many early Victorian boxes, both have a flap behind the (in this instance vertical) posting aperture. The makers were Andrew Handyside & Co of Derby, but as is the case with much street furniture successive painting has blurred the name and other detail.

One of the many attractions of Eton in Berkshire is this fluted pillar box that stands beside the High Street. Dating from about 1856, the box was manufactured by Smith & Hawkes of Birmingham. There are 16 flutes, and the door to the interior is unusually placed at the back of the box. A weather flap is located behind the narrow vertical posting slit around which in very small letters appear the words 'Letter box'. A similar, but renovated, box may be seen in Banbury, Oxfordshire.

Sadly in need of painting when this photograph was taken was the rare letter box in World's End, Hampshire. It was made by Cochrane & Co of Dudley, and dates from 1859. Both the makers' name and the date appear very clearly on the black-painted base.

It will be noted that the box bears no royal cipher, nor any cast legend to connect it with the Post Office. Like the 'Penfold' boxes (page 110) it possesses a horizontal flap in the posting aperture, and its top is markedly similar to those of the Liverpool boxes produced a few years later (page 109).

Liverpool was unique in possessing its own exclusive type of letter box, but unfortunately few now remain on the streets. The boxes were manufactured by Cochrane & Co of Dudley and were brought out in 1863. Distinctive features include their girth, and the surmounting crown peculiar only to these boxes. Unlike some Victorian boxes the one shown here has no weather flap behind its horizontal posting aperture. The box stands at the kerbside, as do many pillar boxes, but somewhat inconveniently faces into the busy Sheil Road.

Among the more attractively designed letter boxes introduced during Queen Victoria's reign were the hexagonal ones named after their designer J. W. Penfold. They were produced during the 1860s and 1870s by several companies including Cochrane Grove & Co of Dudley.

Lone 'Penfold' boxes are to be seen in a number of places, such as Buxton, Cambridge and Truro; but Cheltenham is outstanding in possessing at least six. That shown here is situated in Douro Road, Cheltenham.

In Lower Winchendon, Buckinghamshire, a wall box made by W. T. Allen & Co of London has been set into a distinguished stone and mortar pillar surmounted by a ball. It stands within a small grassed triangle near the centre of the village, and gives the impression that to post a letter here is a dignified and pleasurable act.

Lamp boxes are so named because they were originally designed to be attached to lamp posts. Nowadays they are more likely to be attached to telegraph poles, or to have their own free-standing pedestals.

The practice of fixing a lamp box to a telephone box is peculiar to Scotland. The pair of boxes shown here are situated in Bonjedward, Borders, and it should be noted that both bear the Scottish crown in preference to the coronation crown known as St Edward's, seen in England and Wales. The letter box was made by Carron Company of Carron, Central, Scotland.

The village of Tyneham in Dorset, from which the inhabitants were expelled in 1943 to make way for an army firing range, is now often opened to holidaymakers and other visitors. Apart from encroaching vegetation and some dilapidation, the place remains much as it was when the villagers left for the last time. One consequence of the evacuation has been the fortuitous preservation of the remains of what may be the oldest free-standing telephone box left in Britain. Standing beside the garden wall of a cottage that was once the post office, the box is of precast concrete construction but no longer possesses its door, finial and enamelled roof boards.

Telephone Boxes

The juxtaposition of these telephone boxes in Carey Street, Holborn, London, provides a superlative opportunity for comparison of two successive types of box that were first brought out in the 1920s and 1930s and still remain in use in large numbers.

The taller, and older, box on the left appears to bear no indication as to its makers, but may be by W. Macfarlane & Co Ltd of Glasgow. That on the right was made by Carron Company of Carron. Points for comparison include height, the perforated and cast crowns, the number of glass panes, and the reeding around the door of the older box.

One of a number of precast concrete police telephone boxes on the outskirts of Newport, Gwent. The boxes are topped by a flashable lamp but, unlike their former Metropolitan Police counterparts (see page 118) have not been used as temporary cells.

Telephone Boxes

Edinburgh has been described as the Athens of the North. It is, therefore, not entirely inappropriate that the blue-painted police boxes scattered in and around the city are faintly classical in appearance. Their salient features include decorative wreaths and triangular window panes, whilst some boxes are additionally fitted with a siren on the roof. The box shown here stands in Hunter Square, Edinburgh, and the makers were the Carron Co of Carron, Scotland, a company founded in 1759 and responsible for much street furniture throughout Britain.

It is perhaps not generally realised that the City of London possesses a police force quite separate from that of the Metropolitan area controlled by New Scotland Yard. For use by members of the public and by officers of the force, the City constabulary has set up call posts throughout the City. Each of these posts, painted in various shades of dark or light blue, secretes a telephone for emergency use and has a flashable lamp on its top. This type of call post may also be seen in some provincial towns such as Northampton and Totnes.

To most people the number S63 would mean little, but it is the identification number of the last operative police public call box in the Metropolitan Police area. Once a familiar sight in suburban streets, the majority of boxes of this type were withdrawn about 1969 as ordinary telephones became more numerous and police communication became more sophisticated.

Until its removal in 1980, the sole survivor remaining in service stood beside the A1 road between Stirling Corner and Bignell's Corner, Hertfordshire. Representative of a once-numerous type, the blue-painted, precast concrete box possessed a telephone available for public use, limited accommodation for use as a temporary cell, and on the roof a white lamp that could be flashed to attract the attention of the local patrol.

The Royal Automobile Club (RAC) is Britain's premier motoring organization having been founded, as the Automobile Club, in 1897. The first roadside telephone box for use by members in need of assistance was set up in 1919. Since then the Club has introduced several different types of box. Together they now total about 600 throughout the country.

Whereas the Automobile Association (AA) displays only serial numbers outside its boxes, the RAC has favoured the additional use of placenames. The box shown here, a type dating from about 1930, stands beside the A332 road at Winkfield Row, Berkshire.

Standing close to the 1650 ft (500 m) contour line, this dilapidated AA telephone box number 124 can claim to be one of the most highly situated in the whole of Britain. The box's poor condition may be attributed in part at least to its very exposed position beside the A537 Buxton/Macclesfield road, which can become decidedly hazardous in wintry conditions.

With modern advances in communications systems the multi-wired telegraph pole is becoming a thing of the past. No longer of use, poles are being taken down, and those that do remain are thus increasingly rare. Paired poles are considerably rarer than the single pole, and it is indeed exceptional to find a series of them still in use.

A truly magnificent line of double poles, dated 1908 and 1909, stands alongside the A68 road near Jedburgh in the Borders region of Scotland. Admittedly some take to the fields, but out of a sequence of more than 50 pairs the majority stand actually at the roadside. A number of them are shown here.

Telegraph Poles

Telegraph wires following beside the A68 road south of Jedburgh are obliged to take a sharp bend when the road does likewise. To help negotiate the corner the single pole with jettied crossbars shown here intervenes in a sequence of paired poles standing beside straighter sections of the road.

Scotland, perhaps more than anywhere else in Britain, is a happy hunting ground for the seeker after telegraph poles. Particularly in rural areas, where undergrounding has not been justified, an assortment of poles may be found. Representative of such poles is the well-kept example shown here, which stands beside St Mary's Loch in the Borders region.

Telegraph Poles

In contrast to the many-wired telegraph poles standing alongside the A68 road in Scotland are the poles in rural areas that support only a pair of wires on their way to some isolated farm or house. This example, bearing the number '22' (its height in feet), dates from 1936 and stands near the hamlet of Creeton, Lincolnshire.

The use of corks on telephone wires, although not rare, is nevertheless sufficiently uncommon to merit mention. Their purpose is to emphasize the presence of the wires so that birds may fly clear and escape injury.

The distribution pole shown here from which cork-bearing wires radiate to nearby houses stands in Devonshire Road, Mill Hill, northwest London, and probably dates from about 1936.

Telegraph poles were usually marked to show that they were post office property, to give their date, and sometimes their height in feet or metres.

Despite its great age the clear-cut impression shown here compares favourably with cruder more recent ones. It is borne by a paired pole, now bereft of its many wires, that stands beside the erstwhile B6275 road (now a dead end) near Aldbrough, North Yorkshire.

A rare survival of a once fairly numerous class of enamelled plates attached to telegraph poles as a deterrent (or enticement) to stone-throwers. Coloured red and white, the plate dates from the reign of George V. The date of the pole to which this plate is attached is obscured by the cable guard but it may be of the early or mid 1930s.

If throwing stones at telegraph poles or wires ever grew to be the nuisance that might be inferred from the onetime incidence of these plates, it must surely have been for the perpetrators a rather tame occupation compared with that of smashing street lamps.

Telegraph Poles

In the earlier days of motoring it was the practice for some roadside telegraph poles to be clad in white-painted laths so that they should be seen at night. Such laths are now virtually extinct, their place having been taken by red mounts fitted with 'Wine Gum' type glass reflectors. An example from Northumberland is shown here. These reflectors are in their turn now being superseded by plain red reflective discs of similar diameter.

Although electric trams have long since disappeared from its streets, parts of Nottingham retained in situ an assortment of roadside traction standards of both span suspension and projecting arm types. This ornamented pole is one of a succession standing in Derby Road near the centre of the city.

Trams may come and trams may go but pubs go on for ever!

South End, Croydon, in south London, was served by electric trams from 1901 to 1951. No service trams have been seen there since, but this lone traction pole has been preserved for more than 30 years and now acts as an admirable support for the large pictorial sign of the nearby Swan and Sugar Loaf public house.

One of a series of traction poles lining the sides of Anerley Road, southeast London, which was served by trolleybuses from 1936 to 1959. Whereas the majority of trolleybus poles formerly in the London area have now been removed, this particular route still has them, the attachment of street lights having no doubt contributed to their survival. The poles are painted an unobtrusive grey-green, and noteworthy features include the characteristic ball top and the rake of each pole.

Like any well run transport system, Birmingham Corporation Tramways monitored the timing of its services. To this end about 100 Bundy clocks were set up in various parts of the city in order that tram drivers could record on a tape the times of their arrival. Although no longer used by employees of the present West Midlands Passenger Transport Executive, many of the clocks remain in situ. The posts are painted dark blue, bear the initials BCT, and carry individual serial numbers. In some cases the clock itself has been removed from the post.

The clock shown here is located at a bus turning point in Lanchester Way, Chelmsley Wood.

It is also interesting to note that for such an extensive system the BCT was unusual in having a substandard track gauge of 42 in (1.1 m).

Despite the progressive attitude of London Transport a variety of tram stop flags remained in service right up to 1952, when the last trams were dispensed with. The need for wartime economies no doubt prevented the replacement of obsolescent signs. That shown here is remarkable for the conspicuous use of the word 'cars'.

The city of Birmingham possesses a distinctive style of bus stop flag. The example illustrated here is in Fordhouse Lane, Stirchley. The bracket near the post's base is intended to support a litter bin (in this case absent). In common with the area's Bundy clocks the majority of the posts are painted a dark blue (the 'house' colour of the West Midlands Transport Executive). Others are painted red to signify service by Midland Red buses.

Motor buses first appeared on the streets of Nottingham in 1906. This fading enamelled sign, however, is of a later date.

A bilingual bus stop flag in High Street, Welshpool, Powys.

The history of cabmen's shelters goes back to the days of the hansom cab. Responsibly-minded citizens were then concerned about the behaviour and welfare of cab drivers and so subscribed towards the provision of suitable shelters where the cabbies might rest and eat.

The hansom cab has of course long been replaced by the motor taxi. Shelters have been disappearing steadily. The few now remaining in the streets of London are in a rather decrepit condition.

The shelter shown here stands in Temple Place, Westminster, and conforms to a more or less standard pattern that included green-painted timber construction, a shingled or tiled roof, and louvred ventilation cotes.

One of the best-known seats in the whole of Britain is probably that beneath the open-sided, thatched shelter on the village green in Tolpuddle, Dorset. The shelter was erected in 1934 to commemorate the stand for better working conditions made in 1834 by six labourers who were sentenced to transportation for their actions and became known as the Tolpuddle Martyrs. A beam on the north side of the shelter bears the inscription 'In memory of the Dorset labourers who made a courageous stand for liberty in 1834'.

Northampton is fortunate to possess two highly distinctive former tram passenger shelters dating from about 1920. They are painted a dark blue with small detail picked out in red and white. Regrettably most of the glass panes have been smashed, and it is questionable how much longer the shelters themselves are likely to last. Ideally at least one should be preserved as an example of the work of D. Rowell & Co of London. This company produced a number of different types of shelter the diminishing numbers of which deserve more appreciation than they probably get.

Like the tram passenger shelter in Northampton illustrated on page 139, the iron shelter shown here was made by D. Rowell & Co of London. It was set up in Cosham, Hampshire, for use by tram passengers but since the demise of Portsmouth's tramway system has served as a bus shelter instead.

Since this photograph was taken the shelter appeared to have suffered a little further deterioration but it is to be hoped that it will at least be preserved from further decay, if not restored to its former glory.

Shown here is one of a pair of bus passenger shelters that stand beside the A1 road near Stannington, Northumberland. They are possibly the most beautiful roadside shelters in the whole of Britain and when new would not have disgraced a classical garden. It therefore comes as no great surprise to learn that they were designed by the architect Sir Edwin Lutyens, better known for his work on graceful country houses. The shelters are of white-painted timber and slate and bear the date MCMXXXVII (1937).

Bus passenger shelters are designed for utility rather than beauty. Nevertheless, some local authorities attempt to make the structures visually attractive.

Despite an appearance reminiscent of perhaps a century ago, the brick and thatch shelter in Westcott, Surrey, shown here is not so very old. In fact one of its bricks is inscribed EIIR 1953. Its shape is of interest in that the righthand end is pointed, thereby making it a little easier for someone inside to see the bus approaching. Note also the extra tall belisha beacon.

Some places are less fortunate in their bus shelters than for example, Northampton or Stannington (see pages 139 and 141). This precast concrete example can hardly be described as beautiful. One of a number on the outskirts of Doncaster, South Yorkshire, it presumably affords some protection from bad weather, provided the wind is blowing from a favourable quarter.

The beautiful and historic Holy Island (Lindisfarne) off the coast of Northumberland is joined to the mainland by a sealed road inundated at high tide. For the succour of those unfortunate or foolish enough to become caught by the rising waters, an elevated refuge stands on stilts midway across the causeway. A telephone in the shelter is linked to a local police station in case of need.

The siting of Richmond Bridge over the River Thames has been the subject of controversy both before and since its completion in 1777. The increasing pressure of traffic has been a further cause for concern and led to the eventual widening of the bridge in 1937.

In two pairs of alcoves on each side of the bridge stand iron seats which do not look particularly comfortable and give little opportunity to view the beauties of the river or the bridge itself. The seats are painted black and bear the recurrent legend 'J. & C. 1868 Peirce'.

W. H. Smith, son of the founder of the company of that name and onetime MP for Westminster, donated in 1873 ten seats for public use on the Victoria Embankment, London. The seats were supported by sphinx-like castings. In 1977 the original seats were augmented by copies made by SLB Foundry Ltd of Sittingbourne, Kent, and one of these is illustrated here.

This beautiful seat, supported by two cast-iron kneeling camels, owes its existence to a resolution of 1874 when the Grocers' Company offered to finance the provision of some seats on the Victoria Embankment, London. The seats were manufactured by Z. D. Berry & Son of Westminster, and the records of the Grocers' Company relate its Court's displeasure at a final cost of £270.0.0 for making and installing 12 seats compared with an original anticipated cost not exceeding £100.0.0 for 'some' seats.

Standing beside Andover Road in Cheltenham is a remarkable survival from the early years of the present century. Constructed with glazed earthenware this unusual, hard, and hardly beautiful seat is coloured in brown, green, and ochre, and features animal faces, scrolls, and acanthus-like decoration. Radiating arms divide the seat into four sectors, and a lamp post of more prosaic design rises from the top.

One of an interesting assortment of seats that line the east side of Heath Street, Hampstead, northwest London. Striking features of this type of seat include the constriction of the legs and its unusually generous length of nearly 10 ft (3 m). The six arm rests not only strengthen the seat, but help to separate those not wishing to sit too close to each other. This particular specimen is painted black but others have been seen in white and in light green.

It is no exaggeration to describe the company of Taylor Brothers Ltd as seat-makers to the nation, so widely distributed and readily recognizable are their products. Perhaps rather unexpectedly, few Taylor seats are to be seen in the close vicinity of their home town of Sandiacre, Derbyshire.

Although belonging to a type often used at roadsides, the example shown here was found in a public park in Mill Hill, northwest London. The seat is of a basic style that varies slightly according to locality and ownership. In this case the end carries a cast plate bearing the lamb and flag emblem of the former Hendon Borough Council.

This popular and delicately wrought seat is one of many interesting things to be seen in the town of Ironbridge, Shropshire. It stands at the north corner of the famous bridge from which the place derives its name and affords a good view overlooking the River Severn. A number of similar seats exist in the vicinity and close examination will reveal the name Coalbrookdale, evocative of the ironworks that played an important part in the Industrial Revolution.

The former Great Western Railway, arguably the greatest and most-loved of all railway systems, attracted countless devotees during its existence and aroused a loyalty that continues unabated to this day. Relics of the line are eagerly sought out, and so strong is the affection it engendered that the initials GWR have been interpreted variously as standing for 'God's Wonderful Railway' and 'Gone With Regret'.

A place of pilgrimage for railway and street furniture enthusiasts alike is the village of Adlestrop in Gloucestershire. Prize possessions are a bench embodying the GWR monogram and a nameboard rescued from the now closed local halt. The bench is appropriately painted in brown (the 'house' colours of the GWR were chocolate brown and cream) and bears a poem evocative of rural serenity.

The padlocked gateway to a not-so-public convenience in Circus Place, City of London.

The need to 'spend a penny' is of course not exclusively a British one and increasing use has been made of multilingual signs indicating public conveniences in centres that cater for tourists from many parts of the World. Use is also made of man and woman symbols, but as these are based on Western dress their meaning may not always be clear to peoples of other cultures.

Bristol fashion. Part of the very fine black- and gold-painted enclosure that surrounds the entrance to a now-closed public convenience in Welsh Back, Bristol. Note also the dentated kerbing which is a particular feature of some of the older streets in the city.

A combined ventilator and lamp support standing over an underground public convenience at the junction of Binfield Road and Clapham Road, Stockwell, southwest London. The ventilator is not without decorative features, and it would be interesting to know whether the makers accepted that the panels on the base might be used for the display of posters.

Although the underground lavatory itself is not eligible for consideration its existence does give rise to various fittings above ground that have every right to be regarded as street furniture. Such fittings include lamps, railings, and ventilators. The fine ventilator shown here is in Gracechurch Street, City of London.

For those aware of its existence, this lean-to cast-iron convenience tucked away in Star Yard, Holborn, London, provides a popular and welcome port of call in an area rather bereft of such facilities.

Is this Britain's finest cast-iron loo?

It stands beside Ferry Road in Devonport and is undoubtedly a superb example of a fast-disappearing class of street furniture. It is painted green, and the remarkable external decoration is in very fine condition despite its age. Both patrons and the local authority are to be highly commended for having kept the place in such a good state of preservation. The convenience was made by James Allan Senr & Co of Glasgow, possesses a glazed roof, and houses six patent 'Adamant' stalls.

Although perhaps not so superb as that in Devonport, this cast-iron public convenience tucked into a railway arch beside Landor Street, Birmingham, is certainly more than an 'also ran'. Its interior has been gutted, but it appears once to have contained up to nine stalls. One wonders how many of its former patrons appreciated the fine, green-painted frontage with its discreet screen at the entrance and those magnificent finials.

The Cyclists' Touring Club was founded, as the Bicycle Touring Club, in 1878 and like some of the early motoring clubs it set up warning signs at the roadside to help road-users. The pressed metal signs brought into use by the Club bore the message 'Caution' or 'Danger' or 'To cyclists ride with caution'. It is not known how many of these signs were erected from 1887 onwards, but it is unlikely that more than a very few now survive.

The red and white painted sign shown above stood near the top of a moderately steep and winding hill in southern England.

The New River Company had its origins in the year 1609 when Sir Hugh Myddelton set out to construct an artificial channel to supply London with water. The Company was taken over by the Metropolitan Water Board in 1904. In the vicinity of Ware, Hertfordshire, the channel is crossed by a number of iron bridges dating from 1824 or thereabouts. These bridges were protected from excessive weight (and drivers from nasty accidents) by diamond-shaped warning signs which obviously date from post 1908 and are now rare.

This aged warning sign stands in the north of England. It is unusual, but not unique.

Although many people complain of the proliferation of street signs, the combination here of a bus stop flag with a traffic warning sign (thus avoiding the use of two separate posts) almost certainly renders the latter less conspicuous.

Named after the then minister of transport, Leslie Hore-Belisha, the belisha beacon was officially brought into use in 1934. Since that time it has been much adapted, and provided with hoods, flashing globes, internally-illuminated posts, and emphasis boards (as in the example shown here). With an increase in the use of potentially safer light-controlled pedestrian crossings, there may come a time when the humble belisha beacon becomes redundant and is looked back upon with nostalgia.

This sign, with its typical red ring, is of a class prevalent in the 1930s but now obsolete.

The first electrically-illuminated, but manually-operated, traffic signals in Britain were brought into use at the junction of Piccadilly and St James's Street, Westminster, in 1926. Since that time many different types of signal have been produced by various companies, including The Forest City Signs Ltd. Initially this pioneer company imported signals from America, but began to manufacture them in Britain in the late 1930s. The Forest City signals (now exceedingly rare) are notable for having the word 'Go' on the green aspect. This example was photographed in Northampton.

Unlike the United States or Australia, Britain makes comparatively little use of overhead traffic signals. Single units on cantilevers may be seen near Bagshot, Surrey, and in Holland Road, west London, and a gantry with several units spans part of Coventry Road, Birmingham. Overhead gantries with back-to-back units for tidal flow control of traffic were used in Portsmouth some years ago, but have since been dismantled.

At the time of its erection (1972) the gantry in Torpoint, Cornwall, shown above was unique. It is used for controlling traffic leaving Cornwall by way of the Torpoint ferry. When this traffic becomes heavy it assembles in up to seven lanes (the eighth lane is for emergency use by ambulances etc) and each queue in turn is given a green light to proceed to the waiting ferry.

In Wales in recent years an increasing number of traffic signs have been introduced which bear their message in the Welsh language as well as English. The sign shown here is of additional interest because it gives a rare warning of a tunnel through the northern outskirts of Newport, Gwent.

Roadside signs marking rivers or the boundaries of counties or countries occur in a variety of shapes and sizes. Especially attractive are those near the Welsh border that convey a bilingual welcome to travellers to the Principality.

This example stands on the outskirts of the growing town of Presteigne in Powys.

In the 1850s and 1860s the Corporation of the City of London set up more than 200 plates, posts, and obelisks beside canals, railways and roads, and at sundry other places, to mark the points at which coal being brought into London became liable for tax. It is in the nature of taxes to arouse complaint and that levelled at London's coal tax was that the area of actual liability far exceeded the area of supposed benefit. One of the most northerly of the roadside posts is that shown here, which stands beside the B556 road in Colney Heath, Hertfordshire. The base of the post bears the inscription 'Henry Grissell Regent Canal Ironworks London'.

On the broad pavement outside the Exchange in Bristol, in what was once part of Corn Street but has since been 'pedestrianized', there stands a row of four brass, pedestal-like tables dating from the sixteenth and seventeenth centuries and referred to as 'nails'.

Over these tables deals were done and money paid out by merchants in former times and this custom is reputed to have given rise to the expression 'paying on the nail' meaning paying promptly. The tables are approximately 42 in (107 cm) high and 25 in (63 cm) in diameter.

Standing near the junction of the Promenade and Imperial Square in Cheltenham is this silver-painted, perforated post, the appurtenance to an underground ventilating shaft. It is not uncommon for some items of street furniture to harbour or support others; in this case the opportunity has been taken of attaching to the post a litter basket.

Peculiar to Bristol are the kerbside ventilators that occur in a variety of colours, heights, and styles. A stranger to the city might think them to be sewer ventilators, but in fact they are air vents serving electricity sub-stations or underground ducts. Many, if not all, of the vents bear a label with the name of the street in which they stand, as does this blue-painted vent in Queen Charlotte Street.

Advertisement hoardings have been with us for years, but a more recent introduction has been the pavement pillar. Of the several designs in current use this one in Royal Parade, Plymouth, is particularly attractive. Quite a number of such pillars stand on the pavements of the city centre, and with their domed tops give distinction to the area.

At the onset of World War II air raid sirens were set up throughout the country to warn of the approach of enemy aircraft and to sound an 'all clear' when the danger was judged to have passed.

Though some sirens were located on the roofs of police stations or other buildings, the majority were probably mounted on roadside poles approximately 40 ft (12 m) high. Like the example at Kelly's Corner, northwest London, shown here, many of these have been retained in situ and are now painted green as distinct from their wartime colours of red and silver. The peacetime roles of some sirens include calling out local fire brigade and lifeboat crews, and, in London, warning of flood dangers from the river Thames.

Up to about 1950 some cities and towns in Britain possessed public fire alarms standing on pillars in the street. By breaking the glass and pulling a bar inside, the alarm could be raised in the nearest fire station. These alarms became obsolete as telephones became increasingly common. The city of Liverpool, which withdrew its public alarms in 1969, may have been the last place to do so.

A somewhat similar type of alarm dispensed with the pillar and was instead set in a convenient wall. Both types are now extremely rare. Eton in Berkshire is therefore exceptional in still retaining the example shown here, which is of American manufacture. The renowned Gamewell Corporation can trace its history back to 1852 and the cast-iron box illustrated is of a type that was produced from 1880 to 1920. Traces of the original existence of a glazed keyguard may be seen around the keyhole. Inside the box a hook could be pulled down to send a coded alarm indicating whence it came.

ABBREVIATIONS ON SERVICE INDICATORS

A number of different abbreviations are used on service indicator plates and posts; those most frequently encountered include:

AV air valve
FH fire hydrant
G gas
H hydrant
HB board hydrant
HD double hydrant
HWO hydrant wash-out
SV sluice valve; or, stop valve
V valve
VS valved supply
WM waste meter
WO wash-out
WOH wash-out hydrant

The figures used in conjunction with such abbreviations may indicate some or all of the following: a location or serial number; the size of pipe; the distance of the facility from the indicator and, if applicable, the lateral displacement between the two.

FURTHER READING

Aaron, Henry, *Street Furniture*. Shire, 1980.
Addison, Sir William, *The Old Roads of England*. Batsford, 1980.
Buchanan, R. A., *Industrial Archaeology in Britain*. Penguin, 1972; Allen Lane, 1974.
Dodd, A. E. and E. M., *Peakland Roads and Trackways*. Moorland, 1974.; paperback 1982.
Farrugia, Jean Y. *The Letter Box: History of Post Office Pillar and Wall Boxes*. Centaur Press. 1969.
Richardson, John, *The Local Historian's Encyclopaedia*. Historical Publications, 1974.
Robertson, Patrick, *The Shell Book of Firsts*. Michael Joseph, 1974.

INDEX